A Note to Parents

DK READERS is a compelling program for beginning readers, designed in conjunction with leading literacy experts, including Dr. Linda Gambrell, Distinguished Professor of Education at Clemson University. Dr. Gambrell has served as President of the National Reading Conference, the College Reading Association, and the International Reading Association.

Beautiful illustrations and superb full-color photographs combine with engaging, easy-to-read stories to offer a fresh approach to each subject in the series. Each DK READER is guaranteed to capture a child's interest while developing his or her reading skills, general knowledge, and love of reading.

The five levels of DK READERS are aimed at different reading abilities, enabling you to choose the books that are exactly right for your child:

Pre-level 1: Learning to read
Level 1: Beginning to read
Level 2: Beginning to read alone
Level 3: Reading alone
Level 4: Proficient readers

The "normal" age at which a child begins to read can be anywhere from three to eight years old. Adult participation through the lower levels is very helpful for providing encouragement, discussing storylines, and sounding out unfamiliar words.

No matter which level you select, you can be sure that you are helping your child learn to read, then read to learn!

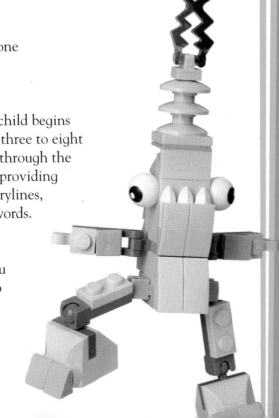

LONDON, NEW YORK, MUNICH,
MELBOURNE, and DELHI

Editor Shari Last
Designer Rhys Thomas
Pre-Production Producer Marc Staples
Producer Louise Minihane
Managing Editor Elizabeth Dowsett
Design Manager Ron Stobbart
Publishing Manager Julie Ferris
Art Director Lisa Lanzarini
Publishing Director Simon Beecroft

Designed for DK by
Thelma-Jane Robb

Reading Consultant
Linda B. Gambrell, Ph.D.

First American Edition, 2014
14 15 16 17 10 9 8 7 6 5 4 3 2 1
Published in the United States by DK Publishing
4th Floor, 345 Hudson Street, New York, New York 10014

001–268992–Sep/14

DK books are available at special discounts when purchased in bulk
for sales promotions, premiums, fund-raising, or educational use.
For details, contact: DK Publishing Special Markets, 4th Floor,
345 Hudson Street, New York, New York 10014
SpecialSales@dk.com

A catalog record for this book is available
from the Library of Congress.

ISBN: 978-1-4654-2455-6 (Paperback)
ISBN: 978-1-4654-2454-9 (Hardcover)

Color reproduction by Alta Image, UK
Printed and bound in China by South China

Discover more at
www.dk.com
www.LEGO.com

Contents

BEGINNING
2
TO READ ALONE

LEGO **Mixels** ™

Let's Mix!

Written by Shari Last

Hello, Mixels™!

Mixels love to sing,
dance, jump, and twirl.
Most of all, they
love to MIX!

Mixels have the most fun when they mix up all their pieces with their friends and combine into something new. Let's mix!

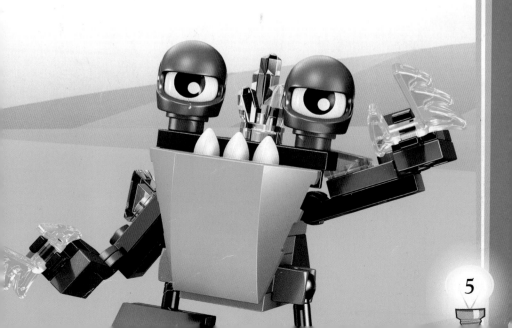

The Frosticons

When Flurr, Slumbo, and Lunk mix, they become icier than ice itself!

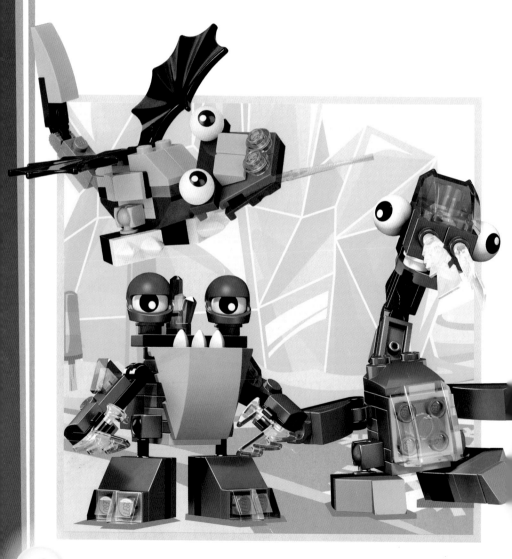

This Frosticons Max has hands that can freeze fire. His breath can turn lava into snow.

Slumbo and his orange friend Balk once mixed together. They didn't expect to grow such a long mustache!

The Infernites

Hello, Flain. Hello, Vulk.
Hello, Zorch. These fiery Infernites
are handy at a barbecue.

When they mix together,
they become this huge Infernites
Max! He has scorching hair and
a red-hot sense of humor.

Time to Mix

Help! Zaptor and Zorch
need to cross the river.
Time to mix!

Now they have Zaptor's energy
and Zorch's firepower to lift off.
They can fly over the river!

The Spikels

Scorpi, Footi, and Hoogi look scary, but they love to hug. They also love to mix.

This big Spikels Max still looks
scary, but he is very gentle.
Just watch out for his spikes!

Hoogi has lots of
fun when he mixes
with his gooey
friend Glurt.
Together, they
become a spiky, slobbering creature.

The Cragsters

The Cragsters are
strong, but slow.
When they need
speed, Krader,
Seismo, and Shuff
mix together!

This big Cragsters Max has
hands that can smash rocks.
His feet are super fast.
No obstacle can slow him down!

The Glorp Corp

Glomp, Glurt, and Torts are ready for the ultimate swamp adventure. Let's mix!

This gooey Glorp Corp Max
leaps over muddy puddles
and swims through swamps.
Goo shoots from his fangs!
The next adventure
will be a slimy one!

The Wiztastics

Wizwuz, Mesmo, and Magnifo
love doing magic tricks.
Their magic show is
the greatest in the land.

When they mix, they become this flying Wiztastics Max. He can do any magic trick you want.

Magnifo likes to mix with his slimy friend Glurt. It helps Magnifo think up exciting new magic tricks.

Silly or Quiet?

Glomp and Mesmo
are very different.
Glomp loves
playing silly games.

Mesmo is a
lot quieter.

When Glomp and Mesmo mix,
they make up a game to play
together. It is silly AND quiet.
Perfect!

The Fang Gang

Oh dear.
Chomly
is hungrier
than ever!

Jawg and Gobba
want to help. MIX!

This hungry Fang Gang Max
can find the best food around.
His huge teeth chomp through
anything. Dinner time!

The Electroids

How many Electroids does it take to change a light bulb? Three! Teslo, Zaptor, and Volectro.

When they mix, they become a
crazy, crackling Electroids Max.
Now they are tall enough
to reach the light bulb.

Teslo and Krader like
mixing together.
They smash lots of rocks
with their amazing
lightning-smash power!

The Flexers

Who is this bug-like Mixel?

He is what you get when
Tentro, Kraw, and Balk mix.

This big, cheerful Flexers Max
loves climbing walls and
bouncing from place to place.

Quiz

1. What color are the Frosticons?

2. Which Mixels are fiery?

3. Which Mixel likes mixing with his gooey friend Glurt?

4. Which Mixels can smash rocks?

5. Which Mixels are ready for a swamp adventure?

6. Which Mixels love doing magic tricks?

7. Which Mixel is hungrier than ever?

8. What kind of Mixel is Gobba?

9. What kind of Mixels are Teslo, Zaptor, and Volectro?

10. What color are the Flexers?

Answers on
page 31

Glossary

bug-like
looks like a bug

combine
mix together

fiery
something
made of fire
or flames

lava
hot, melted
rock

magician
someone who
performs magic

mustache
hair that grows
under your nose

obstacle
something that
gets in your way

scorching
extremely hot

slobbering
dribbling

swamp
an area of wet,
muddy land

ultimate
the best

Index

Answers to the quiz on pages 28 and 29:
1. Blue 2. The Infernites 3. Hoogi 4. The Cragsters
5. The Glorp Corp 6. The Wiztastics 7. Chomly
8. A Fang Gang Mixel 9. Electroids 10. Orange

Here are some other DK Readers you might enjoy.

Level 2

LEGO® Legends of Chima™: Tribes of Chima
Enter the mysterious land of Chima and discover the amazing animal tribes who live there.

LEGO® Friends: Perfect Pets
Learn all about Mia, Olivia, Andrea, Stephanie, and Emma's pets—and discover how much fun pets can be!

Star Wars Rebels™: Meet the Rebels
Meet the *Star Wars Rebels* heroes and learn all about the enemies from the evil Empire they are rebelling against.

Level 3

LEGO® Legends of Chima™: Heroes' Quest
Who are the mysterious Legend Beasts? Join the heroes of Chima on their quest to find these mythical creatures.

LEGO® Friends: Summer Adventures
Enjoy a summer of fun in Heartlake City with Emma, Mia, Andrea, Stephanie, Olivia, and friends.

Angry Birds™ *Star Wars*®: Lard Vader's Villains
Discover a band of nasty villains! Meet Lard Vader and the Empire Pigs as they try to take control of the galaxy.